PRACTICAL ELMAN HYPNOTHERAPY

Applications in Rapid Hypnotherapy

Tim Brunson, PhD

Disclaimer

The content of this book is intended solely for the use of clinicians involved with various integrative medical disciplines. This book is not intended for the general public. Clinicians using the content contained herein take sole responsibility for any claims arising from this material.

The International Hypnosis Research Institute, LLC

600 Leighton Avenue, Suite C

Anniston, Alabama 36207

http://www.hypnosisresearchinstitute.org

CONTENTS

INTRODUCTION

This book will cover several of the applications for Elman's various techniques.

HYPNOANALYSIS

Elman called hypnoanalysis the ground jewel of hypnosis. He would use a somnambulistic trance to regress the patient back to an event which would trigger a neurotic emotion. In turn this could cure several illnesses to include migraines, stuttering, and many others. The goal is to find repressed memories, which are then brought to the surface. His belief was that a repressed memory could be recalled and then used to prevent the re-occurrence of the ailment.

Hypnoanalysis was discovered by Sigmund Freud, who gave up on this due to problems with his speed of inducing hypnosis. Elman was a friend of Freud's nephew, who was the source of Elman's information. Using the methods popular in his day, Freud took two to three hours to induce the level of hypnosis required to do this analysis. Nevertheless, Elman believed that Freud would have had a preference for hypnoanalysis, but abandoned it for psychoanalysis, which he felt was more practical.

As a therapist, often you will be surprised when you find out the root causes of a patient's emotional problems. This could have dramatic results. However, care should be taken to fully uncover all the memories related to the ailment. Some of these memories may be symbolic. An example of this would be a concern that a current or ex-husband symbolized a man who raped the patient during her childhood years. Also, once the traumatic experience is uncovered, then all characteristics of the memory must be examined. The incidents of the ailment's occurrence will contain these characteristics. This is not a simplistic technique and should only be used by clinicians who are properly trained and licensed. Sometimes when a person remembers the incident, an abreaction can occur. The therapist must be prepared to handle this if it happens.

Note that unlike the rest of Elman's techniques, a hypnoanalysis session may take an hour or more. Also, he warned that this will not work with resistant patients. Elman said that hypnoanalysis should be used as an adjunct to the hypnosis process.

MIGRAINES

In one of his classes, Elman performed a hypnoanalysis with a lady who had suffered from migraine headaches for over 20 years. His goal was to search for the cause of her problem.

What he uncovered before the hypnotic trance induction was that when she was seven years old, she witnessed her younger sister being abused by a knife welding young man. He threatened the patient that if she told anyone, he would come back and hurt the younger girl. While it may have been obvious that this was the triggering event, Elman wanted to place the patient into a somnambulistic trance where this could be confirmed.

Here's what happened:

"Take a long, deep breath and close your eyes. Now relax and let every muscle in your body go limp. And, let your eye muscles relax to the point where they just won't work. Now, take a long deep breath and let every muscle relax. Let your level of relaxation just double. Now test

your eye muscles and make sure that they won't work. Let that feeling go right down to your toes. Now I know that you are relaxed. I'm going to pick up your hand. Yes, your arm is as limp as a dishrag. As I let it go, you will go even deeper into relaxation. Now we have the physical relaxation we want, let's get mental relaxation. Now count from one hundred backwards. With every number your re-laxation will double. And when you get to 98 there will not be any numbers. Let them disappear. 100. Now let them disappear. 99. Double your relaxation. 98. Now they are all gone. Now everything you have forgotten and every-thing you remember in your life is just a memory. And in fact, everything in your life that you've ever done is a part of you. It exists as part of you. And when you are in the state you are now; we can take you back to any part of your life. And you can live it all over again."

"And when I snap my fingers you will be back in the first grade. It will be so clear because you will BE there. You will see the teacher; you see the children. You'll walk over to the window and see just what you see when you are in the 1ˢᵗ grade. One, two, three." SNAP. *"You are back in the first grade. Did you like your teacher.?* **Yes***. And the little boy sitting near you, what is his name?* **Ben***. And how are things at home?* **Fine***. Do you know what a headache is?* **No***."*

"Now I'm going to snap my fingers and you are going to be in the third grade." SNAP. *"Do you like the third grade?*

Yes. Good. Tell me, do you have to take care of your sister much? **Not much. I sometimes wait on her.** *And, how is she?* **She is better.** *When you were in the 2nd grade, something happens. Have you ever told anyone?* **No.** *Have you ever seen him?* **Yes.** *Were you scared of him?* **No.**"

"*I'm going to snap my fingers and take you back to right after the incident. I want you to see him just for an instant. Then I'm going to take him away.*" SNAP. "*He is there. Now, I'm going to take him away. When you saw him, where you scared?* **Yes, I was frightened for my sister.** *You never told anyone, so you wouldn't have much reason to be frightened for your sister. Were you frightened for yourself?* **No.**"

"*I'm going to snap my fingers and you will be in the fourth grade.*" SNAP. "**I like school.** *How do you get along with your mother?* **Okay.** *And your daddy?* **Okay.**"

"*Let's take you to the eighth grade.*" SNAP. "*Did you have a headache when you were in the eighth grade?* **Yes.** *I'm going to snap my fingers and you are going back to right before you had your first headache.*" SNAP. "*Where are you?* **I'm getting ready to sing. I like the song. Then I get sick.** *Now when I snap my fingers, I want you to go right before you got sick.*" SNAP. "**I like the song.** *What else?* **We are getting ready to move. I'm getting frightened.** *Now I'm going to take you to five seconds before the headache* *started. **I like the school. I don't want to move**.*"

While the patient was still in the somnambulistic state, Elman uncovered that she was afraid to talk to her mother about her concerns regarding the move. She was afraid of losing security and losing her friends. But she wanted to move. This was a conflict between her desires and what she wanted to do. This was the triggering event. Elman then took her to her second headache.

THE EXTRACTION OF DREAM MATERIAL

During hypnoanalysis, Elman also asked his patients to regress to a particular dream. While the patient was reliving the dream, he would then get them to discuss the content. And then later he would induce a sleep state and give them the suggestion that they would again have a dream which had previously occurred. He would talk to the patient using the phrase, *"You will stay asleep, but you will hear my voice and you won't wake up."* Next, he would say, *"I will snap my fingers and you will be able to tell me the meaning of the dream."* If the patient had a difficulty speaking or had a problem explaining the meaning, then he would again suggest that the difficulty would go away. If this did not work, he would use ideomotor responses to explore further. The extraction of dream material is used as an adjunct to hypnoanalysis. The intent is to uncover the traumatic event which triggered a neurotic emotion.

STUTTERING

Elman would use hypnoanalysis to discover the roots of stuttering. Stuttering is an effect, not a cause. Therefore, the therapist needs to get back to the cause. With this problem, the patient normally had a situation in his life where he had to talk but did not want to talk. Normally, stutterers are sent to speech therapists. They can teach someone to speak clearly, but very slowly and unnaturally. They do not address the cause.

In one example, Elman performed hypnoanalysis with a 10-year-old child who had been stuttering for a long time. He took him back to two years of age when the stuttering began. During trance the child remembered pulling a vase off a table. The vase smashed on the floor. Although this seemed to be the root of the stuttering, it was not. When the child was one year old, he pulled his uncle's birthday cake onto the floor. His aunt laid into him. However, stuttering did not happen until after the vase incident.   The first incident scared the kid, but the second incident apparently caused the stutter. Elman took child back to several incidents. What he discovered was a little more complex. The boy had been raised by his aunt as he was born out of wedlock and his mother was not able to raise him. Then at age two, his mother takes him from his aunt. It was that event that led to the stuttering.

The traumatic event which triggers a neurotic emotion related to an illness is like a cry below consciousness. This can cause illnesses such as asthma, tics, allergies, and others. The abreaction caused by a revivication will act as cleansing intervention. Again, hypnoanalysis should only be performed by a therapist who is adequately experienced and licensed. Beyond the legality issue, there is a probability that an abreaction may re-traumatize the patient and do further harm. I recognize that there are several professionals, such as law enforcement, firemen and other first responders who display talent working with abreactions. And, I believe that all hypnotherapists should have the requisite skills to work with this phenomenon. However, regardless of the competency, care must be taken to assure that any clinician performing hypnoanalysis respects legal limitations.

CHILDBIRTH

Several times in this series I have talked about issues concerning the use of Elman techniques for assisting a woman as she prepares for childbirth. I have exhaustively discussed hypnotic coma and then I later covered hypnosis related to the sleep state. Both below-somnambulism levels can be successfully used for childbirth preparation. If the clinician has a choice, the level of hypnosis related to sleep is the best method to use. A deeper level of anesthesia can be achieved with this technique. And, the post hypnotic suggestions given are often much more powerful. The goal is to give the expectant mother a suggestion that she would have local anesthesia as appropriate for the delivery. This would allow her to be fully aware and able to enjoy watching the birth. Also, this has the advantage of making the contractions much more comfortable. Elman believed that the contractions were 25% more effective than normal. Conversely, the use of hypnosis, which most definitely would work for childbirth, would leave the patient so relaxed that the clarity of experience would be unhampered.

When preparing a patient for childbirth, it is advisable for her to be prepared with a cue word which can be given by the doctor to trigger local anesthesia. This post hypnotic suggestion could be given by the doctor over the phone. Also, Elman suggested that should the doctor not be available, he would install a second word which the patient could give herself. (The intent is to install this post hypnotic suggested word so that it could only be triggered by the doctor or the patient.)

IDEOMOTOR RESPONSE

An ideomotor response is a subconscious signal which a subject in a hypnotic trance gives indicating an idea or thought. There are times when the patient may be reluctant to speak, or there may be a difficulty getting the patient to access deeply repressed materials. Of course, I'm assuming that subject is in a somnambulistic or below trance state.

The word aphasia means the inability to speak. Beware, because aphasia can also happen in a light hypnotic state and is then called false somnambulism.

In the recordings of his original courses, I have heard Elman use ideomotor responses when he taught and demonstrated hypnoanalysis, the elicitation of dream material, and hypnosis related to sleep. As the purpose of hypnoanalysis is to detect repressed memories and derive their meanings so that a neurotic emotion can be neutralized, without the ability to elicit ideomotor responses it would be difficult for the operator to get the necessary responses. This extends to cases where the elicitation of dream material is used as part of the hypnoanalysis process. When ideomotor responses are solicited during hypnosis related to sleep, Elman often solicited a signal to confirm that the sleeping person could still hear him.

Those familiar with forensic hypnosis should have been trained in the use of ideomotor responses. For instance, if after inducing somnambulism you are attempting to get a witness to remember a license plate or some detail about a vehicle or a suspect, ideomotor responses are great. Let me give you an example of instructions which I would use with a forensic hypnosis subject.

"If your subconscious mind wishes to signal 'Yes', please raise your right index finger. If your subconscious mind wishes to signal 'No', please raise your left index finger. If your subconscious mind does not know the answer, make no signal." While I would do this prior to the forensic induction as it would appear to the court and the opposing attorney that I was not giving questionable suggestions to the witness while under trance, an ideomotor response suggestion may also be given while the subject is in somnambulistic or below states. When Elman was having difficulty with a patient undergoing hypnoanalysis, he would promptly suggest that if a con-

dition existed, she should signal by raising a finger. For non-forensic work, this is quite acceptable.

IMPOTENCE, FRIGIDITY AND STERILITY

When working with sexual problems, all clinicians must be sure that physical pathologies have been ruled out by competent medical practitioners.

Elman claimed that he was extremely successful with impotence problems. He found that there are two types of cases. The first is with a man who consciously knows the cause or causes. Typical causes could be guilt, child abuse or feelings of inadequacy. In these cases, the therapist can give superficial suggestions that the impotence will go away and that the patient would be able to perform adequately. This would be done while the patient was in deep somnambulism. The second happens when the patient does not know the cause at a conscious level. Even though Elman was successful with some of these, he said that this was only a temporary result. In these cases, Elman recommended the use of hypnoanalysis. Once this is accomplished and the cause is found, then the superficial suggestions given in deep somnambulism will work.

Elman was much more successful with impotence problems than with frigidity. This was because women may have problems talking to men about intimate sexual problems. Therefore, he was only successful with about 6 out of 10 patients. He said that if the problem is known at the conscious level, then superficial suggestions under somnambulism will work. Again, if the cause is not known, then hypnoanalysis is indicated. Elman said that frigidity is extremely common.

Elman maintained that patients with frigidity must be handled with finesse since it is a very intimate problem. Doctors and therapists must avoid common words such as intercourse. If you use words like union, then you would find the patient's sensibilities would not be offended.

In one difficult case, it came out during the hypnoanalysis that the patient had been raped when she was eight. She finally admitted that whenever her husband approached her for the purpose of consummation, she tensed up because he triggered the memory of the rapist. Once this was determined, Elman was able to give her suggestions which resolved the issue.

During his discussion of the case, Elman made an interesting point. When the patient began abreacting painfully, he ceased asking her what was happening now, and to tell him what happened then. This effectively dissociated the patient from the incident.

Elman addressed dyspareunia with his physician students. This is painful sexual intercourse, which is believed to be due to medical or psychological causes. This is normally reported exclusively by women. Like impotence and frigidity problems, if the cause can be consciously expressed, the superficial suggestions under somnambulism are indicated. Otherwise, hypnoanalysis should be used.

PAIN

Anything that can be produced by suggestion can be removed by suggestion. This includes pain. Techniques like hypnotic coma, hypnosis related to the sleep state, and even waking hypnosis, or superficial suggestions in somnambulism can be extremely helpful in removing pain. In this book series I have given several examples of hypnosis creating both general and local anesthesia.

When Elman was eight and a half years old, his father was dying of cancer. A stage hypnotist, who was a friend of his father, was able to use hypnosis to alleviate the pain. This allowed his father to at least be able to talk to his family prior to his death.

Elman had several students who worked with cancer patients. The use of his techniques to alleviate the cancer-related pain was common among them. Many of them claimed that their patients would need absolutely no chemical relief. Elman used the hypnotic coma technique for getting rid of intractable pain.

He also talked about how patients can hold on to pain even after chemical anesthesia had been administered. This happens a lot with dentists and medical doctors doing tonsillectomies. Usually fear alone is the reason for a patient to hold onto pain. If fear is not the only factor, then there must be another. In these cases, hypnoanalysis is indicated as the technique to find and eliminate the underlying cause.

During child delivery, if the patient has not been totally sedated, she can be given suggestions between contractions that the next contraction can be easier and easier. This will help the patient handle the pain. Again, the more confident the hypnotic operator is, the more likely the patient will find that the pain of the contractions will reduce.

Don't be surprised if you need to renew suggestions of anesthesia frequently. Even the use of chemical pain medication must be given recurrently. Hypnotic suggestions are no different.

PREGNANCY REJECTION

Elman's students had mixed results using suggestions under somnambulism to prevent pregnancy rejection. Some students claimed that they had hundreds of patients who were successful with this problem when they used hypnosis. Others claimed to have had absolutely no success.

Pregnancy rejection does not mean that the patient does not want the child. However, problems like a pending divorce, arguments, and other worries may cause the rejection. Normally, vomiting and nausea occur. Often, when you see the signs of rejection and superficial suggestions fail to work, then hypnoanalysis should be used. Once the underlying worries, fears or causes are determined, then addressing the problem by suggestion under somnambulism can normally resolve the problem.

ILLNESSES

Back in the 1950's, Elman asked his students if they felt that their patients nominated their illnesses. Do we make our illnesses possible?

Many respected doctors told Elman that all illnesses are rooted in emotion. These findings were not published at that time. Elman would say that certain ailments are caused by emotions and all neuroses are created by emotions.

He felt that we have much more control over a lot of physiological processes than we think. Furthermore, he said that with hypnosis you can never mask a symptom; you can alleviate a symptom, but not mask it. Nevertheless, he admitted that there were several people in the medical profession who believed that hypnosis could cure ailments. Research by Dr. Joe Dispenza regarding terminally ill patients who went into remission supports this view. So does recent research showing that wounds can heal faster if hypnosis is used.

Elman discussed our ability to control our blood flow. If you are familiar with biofeedback training or autogenics, you should be comfortable with our ability to control the warmth or coolness of our extremities. Just think of mood rings, which have been advertised to reveal someone's emotional attraction to others. Actually, these devices respond to the peripheral warmth resulting from parasympathetic activation rather than feelings of affection.

Suggestion in somnambulism and during waking hypnosis can control all blood flow other than arterial bleeding. This is extremely useful during medical situations. This is also a very useful skill for emergency medical technicians who respond to traumatic accidents.

PRE-OPERATIVE TALKS

This is a pre-operative talk as taught by Elman:

"My name is Doctor Jones. I will be in charge of your surgery in the morning. And, I know that everyone who is facing a surgery has a little apprehension and fear. And, I would like to help you get past that. For instance, I know that you can have a good night sleep tonight. So, I'm going to show you how to relax. And, even when it comes to the operation, I'm going to show you how to relax. Take a good, long deep breath. Let me have your hand. Now, I'm going to bring my hand down like this. Just close your eyes. Now relax those eye muscles to the point where they just won't work. Now when you are sure that they won't work, let that feeling go right down to your toes. Now feel that relaxation. And, when I lift your hand and drop it your relaxation will go so much deeper. That's right. And when you're relaxed like this, you can tell how much more relaxed the operation will be for you. Let me tell you some of the advantages of your relaxation. When we enter the operating room like this, you will need much less anesthesia, and you

will have better anesthesia. And another thing that will happen is that you will have quicker post-operative recovery. You'll get well so much faster. Now there are certain things that we should tell you to dispel your fears. Surgery is not what it once was when they took you into an operating room and did the operation. Today we have to know that the body can stand the operation. That is the purpose of all the tests they've been doing the past 24 hours. We know that your body is able to stand the operation and it will be much easier than you think it will. You'll find that the post-operative will be much easier and that you won't have any discomfort at all. And, you will feel so good after the operation is over. Now in the morning when I see you in the operating room, I'll tell you to close your eyes. And, when you do you will be just as relaxed as you are right now. And the operation will be so easy for you. And when you wake up, you'll be back in your room recovering. You'll feel so good because everything that was troubling you will have been fixed and you will be back on your way to health. And one very important thing that you must know, and we must know, do you have any mental reservations? You must tell me now. If there is anything that we have to, talk about, let's talk about them now." (The patient says that there is nothing on her mind.) *"Now in the morning, when I ask you to close your eyes you will feel as relaxed as you are now. Now open your eyes. How do you feel?"*

When Elman suggested that the doctor ask the patient if there is anything on her mind, this is where he would learn about morbid fears or a will to die. He said that if this is discovered, it should be converted immediately to a will to live. If not, the surgery should be postponed.

STAGE FRIGHT

Most performers use some form of autosuggestion to handle the anxiety and excitement associated with public speaking or any type of stage performance. Using the autosuggestion technique with affirmations about confidence, you can remember information or lines and get into the positive state needed to give a fantastic performance. Waking hypnosis can also be used. However, Elman preferred either autosuggestion or a trance state. In the latter, the somnambulistic subject would be given the same suggestions just mentioned. It is also important to give a post hypnotic suggestion very similar to the one which I presented for the pre-operative talk. Merely suggest that before they go to the podium or onto the stage, they close their eyes and return to the confident state suggested during the hypnosis. Using various methods of hypnosis to reframe anxiety into excitement is quite powerful.

You can also use suggestion under somnambulism to get rid of headaches. This is a matter of finding the cause of the headaches. As discussed previously, Elman used hypnoanalysis to remove the cause of migraine headaches. However, for headaches other than migraines, the use of suggestions under somnambulism can work in many cases. Realize that headaches have a cause. If the patient is aware of the cause, then the use of hypnoanalysis is not required. It is merely a matter of disconnecting the cause from the headache using suggestion. Remember that headaches are like any other pain in that it may be a signal that a medical issue must be investigated and treated.

CONCEPT OF THE SEAL

Lastly, I want to discuss the concept of the "seal." This is a technique when the hypnotic operator gives the subject a post hypnotic suggestion that they would not be able to achieve a trance state unless they were induced or triggered by a specific operator. Elman highly objected to doing this as it could prevent the subject from receiving the benefit of hypnosis from another party. Frankly, I agree with Elman.

SUMMARY

Over the years I have attended a few classes and courses in Elman hypnotherapy. Their quality and scope varied. Only one instructor, Gerald Kein, presented a true understanding of Elman's work. The major shortfall of most of the other instruction was that it was limited to teaching the route mechanics of the Elman technique without a substantial understanding of the essence of his philosophy of hypnosis.

During this project I have been impressed with both the complexity and simplicity of Elman's work. It has covered a wide range of techniques and applications. The Elman technique was merely one of them. Then it becomes simplistic in that once you fully understand that hypnosis is a condition of the bypass of the critical faculty and the suspension of selective thinking, you can truly understand that this is the root of his entire approach. This gives the operator the flexibility to innovate beyond what is too often taught as a rigid approach. In short, it is not the step-by-step protocol that is as important as the two fundamental requirements.

When trancework is used to get the subject into a state where there is sufficient bypass of the critical faculty, the operator must assure that there is sufficient depth. Every technique and application requires a minimum somnambulistic state. Physical relaxation regardless of the intensity is not enough unless mental relaxation is also present. In turn, mental relaxation is required to be tested with some form of amnesia. This is tested by suggesting that the subject forget some easily remembered item such as a sequential number, address, name, or telephone number. If amnesia is not achieved, the operator has probably induced a light trance. Aphasia, which is defined as an inability or unwillingness to speak, is not a sign of somnambulism. If working with a trance state, the operator must not proceed.

While the seven-step classic Elman technique is highly effective, he taught that anything can create trance. He called this the "catalyst method". Again, the goal is to rapidly introduce the subject to a state of somnambulism without going through all the ritual.

Additionally, waking hypnosis further exemplifies Elman's flexibility and reinforces the fact that a trance state is not required as a condition of hypnosis. This explains the conundrum as to why in an intensely emotional state a suggestion can create a lasting phobia.

Elman pointed out that just about every benefit of a somnambulistic state can be achieved through waking hypnosis. This includes general and local anesthesia.

The two states below somnambulism, which are hypnotic coma and hypnosis related to the sleep state, offer two additional and profound conditions which are highly affective for anesthesia. These are rarely taught in many Elman courses. However, they are very simple extensions of the somnambulistic state.

Lastly, I covered several other techniques which are variations. Yet, they inevitably rely on the two central requirements. Then I covered several behavioral and medical applications to include the lengthy form of psychoanalysis called hypnoanalysis.

Once Elman hypnotherapy is understood and either incorporated in a clinical practice and/or used as a complement to other skills such as guided imagery or Ericksonian hypnosis, the practitioner will increase his ability to use the mind/body continuum to further the healing process. When this is achieved, the clinician will truly understand that the root of all healing resides in the mind and body of the subject.

ABOUT THE AUTHOR

In addition to degrees in political science, economics, management, finance, and strategic studies, Dr. Tim Brunson, has received a Doctor of Clinical Hypnotherapy and a Doctor of Philosophy Clinical Hypnotherapy degrees. He has practiced nearly three decades with clients and patients as well as taught medical, dental, and mental health clinicians from around the world. His quest to understand human individual and group transformation has led him to study a wide range of fields to include Artificial Intelligence, neurology, and a wide range of mind/body modalities. He has studied with numerous thought leaders in those fields. He has a background in the mental training included in Vajrayana Buddhism and has taken instruction from the 14th Dalai Lama and several abbots and notable authorities. He is the developer of both the Neurology of Suggestion and Advanced Neuro-Noetic Hypnosis.

RESOURCES

General:

The International Hypnosis Research Institute

IHRI membership

Advanced-Neuro-Noetic-Hypnosis

Courses

Books, E-Books, And Audiobooks:

Sets

Elman Hypnotherapy: Beyond the Basics

Improving Your Performance Genius

Enhancing Performance: Unleashing Your True Potential (Bundled)

Innovations in Mind/Body Therapies

The Mind/Body Connection

The New Biology

The Neurology of Mind/Body Health

Transformation Revisited

The Immune System Primer

Using Imagery to Heal

A Quick Pain Management Primer

Healing the Body Basics

The Mind, Surgery, and Recovery

Calming Your Gut

Innovations in Mind/Body Therapies (Bundled)

The Neurology of Suggestion Series

The Neurology of Suggestion

Advanced Hypnotherapy Protocols and Applications

The Neurology of Suggestion Series (Bundled)

The Neurology of Suggestion Basics

Change: A New Paradigm for Transformation

Brain Potential: Enhancing and Inhibiting for Peak Performance

Reshaping: Changing your Brain and Body

Individual Books

Advanced Hypnotherapy Script Writing Techniques

Clinical Hypnotherapy Fundamentals

Healing the Body

Healing the Mind

New Directions in Hypnotherapy

Rapid Change: The Secrets of Lasting Personal and Group Transformation

Space/Time-based Interventions: Simple techniques that enhance hypnotherapy

www.ingramcontent.com/pod-product-compliance
Lightning Source LLC
Chambersburg PA
CBHW061532250726
48657CB00005B/2204